D0417677

Building the Global Village

Bruce Kent was active as a Roman Catholic priest for some thirty years until 1987. He is ex-Chair of the Campaign for Nuclear Disarmament, and current President of the International Peace Bureau.

In the series Agenda for the 21st Century

A Future for Socialism (Tony Benn)
Building the Global Village (Bruce Kent)
Green Futures (Sara Parkin)

Agenda for the 21st Century

Building the
Global Village

Bruce Kent

Fount
An Imprint of HarperCollins*Publishers*

First published in Great Britain
in 1991 by Fount Paperbacks

Fount Paperbacks is an imprint of
HarperCollinsRegligious
Part of HarperCollins*Publishers*
77–85 Fulham Palace Road, London W6 8JB

Copyright © 1991 by Bruce Kent

The Author asserts the moral right
to be identified as the author of this work

Printed and bound in Great Britain by
HarperCollins Manufacturing, Glasgow

Phototypeset by Intype, Input Typesetting, London

A catalogue record for this book
available from the British Library

This book is sold subject to the condition that it shall not,
by way of trade or otherwise, be lent, re-sold, hired out or
otherwise circulated without the publisher's prior consent
in any form or binding or cover other than that in which it
is published and without a similar condition including this
condition being imposed on the subsequent purchaser.

Contents

Chapter 1
Optimism and Pessimism

This introduction is not the one I would have written had I started to write this book on time. It was nine months ago, in the spring of 1990, that I began to put these ideas together. That was a good time to look forward in hope. The Cold War was over and the Berlin Wall was down. Mikhail Gorbachev had received his well earned Nobel Peace Prize. The worldwide Green movement had more or less succeeded in turning our minds from individual threats to global ones, ranging from pollution to population, from over-consumption to nuclear accident and the greenhouse effect.

After an appalling forty years the superpower confrontation – the source of a nuclear stalemate in Europe and dozens of wars in the rest of the world – seemed to be over. During those forty years each side had diverted untold billions of dollars and vast amounts of human talent and energy away from the real needs of the human family and towards an unwinnable arms race. Now it seemed that common sense was about to break out. Reason and morality were going to triumph in the end.

Or so it seemed to me and to millions of others. All the talk was of the Peace Dividend – that is, the economic benefits which would result from the ending of the Cold War. It was expected that, as East-West tensions diminished, military budgets and industry would be redirected towards peaceful purposes. When I proposed, at the Labour Party Conference of 1989, a reduction of military expenditure in favour of hospitals, housing, pensions and public transport, there was a wonderfully enthusiastic response. A better world was on the way. In those days I imagined that it would be easy to write this book about the approaching twenty-first century.

It was all too easy. The Gulf Crisis suddenly burst on us and unfolded like some kind of Greek tragedy. By the time this book has been published there may have been some kind of political settle-ment, but it will surely be of a fragile nature.

The crisis has been a dreadful time to live through. We have had to face up to the conse-quences of our arms sales and our economic support for and tolerance of a tyrant whose power we, with the Soviets, the French and the Ameri-cans, helped to build.

In 1982 I was astonished at the speed with

which jingoistic fervour took over during the Falklands war. Those of us who at that time went on believing in negotiations, sanctions and a United Nations settlement were rapidly marginalized. The drums beat, the flags waved and money was suddenly no object. The majority wanted a war, and a victory. The Labour Party jostled with the Conservatives to prove themselves the more patriotic.

I never thought that in less than ten years I would see the whole process start again. But it did. Crude tabloid journalism, endless appeals to patriotism, and manipulation of the United Nations Charter all combined to make war respectable. No one seemed willing to notice that Article 42 of the UN Charter requires the Security Council to consider that sanctions 'would be or have proved to be inadequate' before it can authorize military power. Until dead and mangled civilian bodies began to appear it was hard to call it a war at all. Night after night – and all night for that matter – our TV screens ran a kind of *Star Trek* fantasy, a war devoid of passion and suffering, a war of wonderful technology in which missiles could be popped through front doors and no one seemed to get hurt. The reality was, of course, rather different. It was a war in which the military aims varied almost on a weekly basis and the political future remained totally unclear.

I have had a rude lesson in the absurdity of over-optimism. The twenty-first century is not going to be an entry into Utopia. The crudest ideas about human behaviour are still alive and well. 'I can bash you harder than you can bash me' is still the level of much educated thinking. We are still a long way away from the sort of universalist ideas which sound very nice on *Thought for the Day*. Such beliefs are at best skin deep. Militarily we are highly advanced, but morally we still live in the stone age.

This is therefore a more realistic book than it might otherwise have been. Recent events have shown how little progress we have made in the direction of peaceful internationalism. But being realistic also means that we have to look at the distant horizon to find the road we have to take. That is why I am writing. Whatever the problems, there has to be a vision. Without a vision the people perish.

Chapter 2
New Visions

The Gulf War has reminded me that there are no easy solutions to world problems. If ever there was a situation in which sanctions against an aggressor might have worked, then this was it. Iraq was a country with effectively only one export – oil. Its military machine was largely dependent on spare parts from abroad. Yet sanctions were not given any time to work. For a variety of reasons – emotional rather than rational – war became inevitable. My simple belief in common sense and reason took a heavy blow.

But reduced optimism must mean increased determination. We have to try even harder to change ideas so that people realize how interdependent we all are. We need a revolution in thinking if we are to make sense of the twenty-first century. I don't mean the kind of revolution which just shifts political power around from one group to another. We need a revolution of perspectives. We did not make the planet, we do not own the planet and we have no right to wreck the planet. We are not freeholders, but tenants holding on trust the world in which we live. Irresponsible, greedy and violent, we have brought that world to the brink of destruction. We can blow it apart, pollute it, exploit it and turn it into a desert. Is that the way we want to go on? I doubt it. There is a deep goodness in the human heart and a conscience which will not be silenced.

We are not just entering a new century; we are facing a new world beyond the imagination even of recent generations. The Atlantic can be crossed in a few hours. The Fax machine instantly transmits exact copy to a destination thousands of miles away. The computer in a second can produce total information about anyone on its files. Television brings into our homes not just brutalities in countries on the other side of the world but also the secrets of life under the oceans and in the forests. Never has 'progress' moved so fast, so amazingly, so wonderfully and sometimes so threateningly. We are the first human beings ever to see our planet from the outside – a blue-green globe floating in a sea of dark space. That should inspire wonder and reverence in the dullest heart. In every way we live in a new world of opportunities and threats. We either develop a sense of global community and responsibility, or we carry the mental luggage of the old world into the new one and end up by dishonouring our trust and destroying ourselves and the rest of creation at about the same time.

It is essential that we look again at what we call nationalism. I am no enemy of individual culture, language, history and achievement. God forbid that we ever find ourselves with one standard world culture. Be warned by the onward march of McDonalds and the fast food industry, the ever wider networking of *Neighbours*, the destruction of the countryside worldwide in the name of agribusiness, and the international worship of the car. We are already moving in the direction of a mono-culture. Who can tell one airport duty-free shop from any other?

The move towards one world culture, with English as it language and the television as its symbol, has to be a move backwards and not forwards in human development. Somehow, century after century, we have evolved into different peoples, regions and families. Poetry, history, music, religion, dress, crafts and language all express the wide variety of the human community. If all that were steamrollered into one flat cultural common denominator, it would indeed be a terrible loss.

But the problem that faces us as we move into the next century is how both to preserve variety and to build the global political framework within which that variety can work together for the good of the whole. In the last two centuries we have raised national loyalty above our international loyalty and have assumed that the only proper way for a nation or a people to organize politically is through the sovereign nation state. Of course, the genuinely sovereign state no longer exists, if ever it did. Even the largest states are part of a world economic community which controls them as much as they try to control it. In a world of nuclear and other weapons of terror and mass destruction no state can claim to be sovereign in questions of its own defence. We have created instruments of destruction which threaten us all. Should the calamity of nuclear war ever happen, no state will be able to escape its devastating effects.

It would be absurd to suggest that legitimate patriotism and local loyalty are going to be or ought to be abolished. Different cultures, traditions and languages make life so much more interesting. Who wants some kind of monolithic world state in which all decisions are taken from the centre? On the contrary, power has got to be devolved as widely as possible if people are to have a chance of running their own lives. But the background to the future world political structure has to be that our global unity comes first. Nationalism becomes destructive when it makes the nation the focus of all loyalty. Too often 'my country' becomes more important than 'our world'. No wonder we don't yet realise that the so-called sovereign nation state is not the last word in the political organization of the human community, and that whatever our flag may be, we are all members of one family.

There is a lovely story from the *Hasidim* which is well worth telling. An old Rabbi once asked his pupils how they could tell when night had ended and the day had begun. 'Could it be,' asked one of the students, 'when you can see an animal in the distance and tell whether it is a sheep or a dog?'

'No,' answered the Rabbi.

Another asked, 'Is it when you can look at a tree in the distance and tell whether it's a fig tree or a peach tree?'

'No,' answered the Rabbi.

'Then when is it?' the pupils demanded.

'It is when you can look on the face of any man or woman and see that it is your sister or brother. Because if you cannot see this, it is still night.'

We all find it easy enough to recognize our sisters and brothers when they belong to 'our' country. It is rather more difficult when it comes to foreigners. Is this because of the way in which the world has been divided up into separate nation states?

Chapter 3
The Sovereign Nation State

What on earth is a sovereign nation state? The term is difficult to define, but it might be said to mean a country which does not have to answer to other countries about the management of its own internal affairs and which is in theory independent in its external activity. Most – but not all – nation states have signed the Charter of the United Nations. Not one of them is sovereign in the sense that it has absolute control over its own affairs. Very few of them can claim to contain only one nation. Most states are made up of several nations and in the majority, including Britain, there is tension between one nation and another.

But like it or not, there these states are, right in the centre of our present political world structure. They all have seats and votes in the General Assembly of the United Nations, where in theory they are all equal. However, the existence of the Security Council, in which 'important' states have permanent places and the power of veto, is an acknowledgement of the realities of world power. Not all states are equal.

History has passed this institution down to us. It would, however, be a complete mistake to imagine that no other structure might have been possible, or that we are stuck with the present system for all time. If we are going to move towards the twenty-first century with the global vision that we need, then we clearly have to make some radical changes in our thinking about the political structure of the world.

After all, we human beings have experienced a wide range of political systems through the ages. We have had monarchies and dynasties, empires and commercial federations, city states and feudal power sharings. Territories have been bought, sold, exchanged, conquered and even given as dowries over the centuries. The idea that one defined territory made up a particular country and that within that country there should be one absolute centre of power is quite a new one. King John would not have had so much trouble with his barons if sovereign states had been understood then as they are now.

The nobleman in Bernard Shaw's *St Joan* saw exactly which way history was going. In this dialogue he is talking with his chaplain about an enemy:

Chaplain:	He is only a Frenchman, My Lord.
Nobleman:	A Frenchman: where did you pick up that expression? Are these Burgundians and Bretons and Picards and Gascons beginning to call themselves Frenchmen, just as our fellows are beginning to call themselves Englishmen? They actually talk of France and England as their countries. Theirs if you please. What is to become of me and you if that way of thinking comes into fashion?
Chaplain:	Why my Lord, can it hurt us?
Nobleman:	Men cannot serve two masters. If this cant of serving their country once takes hold of them, goodbye to the authority of their feudal lords, and goodbye to the authority of the church.

Shaw's dialogue is not only about new forms of sovereignty. It is also about the rise of nationalism and of theories about the social contract. According to these theories the power of rulers came from the people. Older ideas about the divine right of kings, about power coming from above rather than from below, were beginning to be widely rejected.

This mix of new ideas – ideas about absolute loyalty to one nation state and about democratic power – did not come to the boil until the time of the French Revolution and Napoleon. Even at that time the idea of a whole country going to war and everybody being involved was still quite a new one. The conscription of young men into the military, which we now think so normal, was then a novel idea. A person's country was becoming the focus of total loyalty in a way that it had not been before.

In our century there have been many who have claimed sovereign independence for every nation. The consequences in terms of further political divisions are clear. Few sovereign states exist today which are not made up of several or even many nations if by a nation one means a group of people united in culture, language, tradition and even religion.

'Every nation has a right to sovereignty,' said the Foreign Minister of Czechoslovakia (newly freed from communism) recently. What can that actually mean? If every nation has such a right, then it has not always been recognized. The response of the English to the nationalist aspirations of the Scots, the Welsh and the Irish hardly points in that direction.

The concept of national sovereignty and the concept of democracy by no means have to co-exist. Dictators can and do play on nationalism as regularly as democrats do.

History and political thinking are ever on the move. No one can say that this or that or the other form of political structure is the only one that we humans can adopt. Local units in an increasingly interdependent world have to be measured, valued and organized in relation to the needs of the whole world community. This is exactly what has not happened. The sovereign state has managed to impose on general thinking the idea that its internal affairs are for it alone to manage, and that its external relationships are not to be measured by universal needs and principles, but are rather to be organized on an *ad hoc* individual treaty basis. Dr Philip Allott of Trinity College, Cambridge, recently made a most interesting comment about international life today: 'It is as if the external life of our societies were still a reflection of the internal life of centuries ago. A fitful struggle among Teutonic Knights or European barons or Chinese feudal lords or Japanese Shoguns. It is as if Thomas Hobbes were the world's only social philosopher.' Hobbes thought of the world, beyond the state, as a dangerous jungle.

It seems to be assumed, in theory at least, that within the sovereign state justice should be seen to be done, the weak should be protected, contracts should be honoured, and ideas about the good of the community should be pursued, but that outside the sovereign state sheer power is what really matters and obligations are to be observed as long as they are convenient.

Most people think this strange idea is normal. It is not normal. It is entirely abnormal. Our human loyalties come in many layers: family, locality, country, culture and world. But we have given to the third of these a near total priority. If we are going to live together in one world and face the challenges of the present and the near future, then we are going to have to think again and make our global unity and its political structure our first concern. The French Jesuit scientist and philosopher, Teilhard de Chardin, wrote:

> *The Age of Nations is past*
> *the task before us now*
> *if we would not perish*
> *is to build the earth.*

Perhaps the era of the sovereign nation state is coming to an end.

Chapter 4
Religions and the Future

People who belong to different religious traditions are often heavily criticized by others working for social change on the grounds that too often religions have made human progress more and not less difficult. Slavery was accepted as normal by religious groups for many centuries. Women have suffered and still suffer marginalization in many societies where religion has been and is influential. Too often the followers of religions have given uncritical support to the wars which their countries have waged. Everyone knows about the dark side of religion. There are few religions that do not have to admit to cruelty, past and present. Religion has often been the flag which has been waved over political differences, as in Northern Ireland and Yugoslavia. Religions have given strong support to state militarism in a variety of ways. Before the plane that dropped the atom bomb on Hiroshima in 1945 took off, a chaplain said a special prayer for the success of the mission and the safe return of the crew. There has been a long and corrupting partnership between Church and State. Take for example this letter written by the Emperor Charlemagne to Pope Leo III in the early Middle Ages:

> It is our part, with the help of Divine Holiness, to defend by armed strength the holy Church of Christ everywhere from the outward onslaught of the pagans . . . it is your part, most Holy Father, to help our armies with our hands lifted up to God like Moses . . .

This was a State/Church partnership which has lasted for centuries. I can say to agnostic and atheist friends that I know as much as anyone else about evils done in the name of religion. But it would be nice if some of the areas of life – law, medicine and education, for instance – in which religion has played a positive and progressive part could also be acknowledged. The faith that launched the Crusades also produced St Francis of Assisi. The age of Cromwell was also the age of the Quaker George Fox.

Moreover, it was our post-religious twentieth century which produced gas chambers and mass extermination. In our nice liberal way we have produced an amoral society in which no-one is really responsible for anything. 'They' somewhere else have to take the blame. J. B. Priestley expressed it very well in a short poem:

> *The real lost souls*
> *Don't wear their hair long and play guitars*
> *They have crew cuts, trained minds*
> *sign on for research in biological warfare*
> *and don't give their parents a moment's worry.*

'It's just like selling cars,' said one of the first directors of the British Defence Sales Organization about arms sales; and in any event he wasn't responsible – it was up to the politicians.

Religions do have positive contributions to make to next-century thinking. To start with, at their best, they have something to say about wealth and power. For example, St Basil the Great wrote:

> When someone steals another's clothes, we call them a thief. Should we not give the same name to one who could clothe the naked and does not? The bread in your cupboard belongs to the hungry; the coat hanging unused in your closet belongs to the one who needs it; the shoes rotting in your closet belong to the one who has no shoes; the money which you hoard up belongs to the poor.

All the major religions are community religions. Individualism is a late Christian aberration. We are trustees of what has been given to us, and accountable for our talents. Our attitude to the world around us should be one of humility, respect and wonder, not one of pride and exploitation – traits which marked our colonial and commercial history so disastrously. Nowhere is this humility better expressed than in Psalm 8 in the Jewish scriptures:

When I see the heavens, the work of your hands,
The moon and the stars which you arranged,
What are we that you keep us in mind,
Human beings, that you care for us?

The best of religion rejects divisions and goes beyond tribal loyalties. The divisions represented by the Tower of Babel would be replaced by the universal message of Pentecost. Race alone was no longer to be the only claim to merit or justification. As Christ said to His disciples, 'I can raise up children to Abraham out of these very stones.' The Good Samaritan who came from an enemy people was a more important figure than the priest who passed by. Christ's message was one of universality, not one of division. Saint Paul puts it most eloquently in his letter to the Galatians: 'There is neither Jew nor Greek, neither slave nor freeman, neither male nor female, for you are all one in Christ Jesus.'

Trusteeship, not exploitation, must be our watchword as we enter the twenty-first century. My inspiration is Christian; let others find theirs where they will. This is not a competition, but a joint journey towards a better kind of world. If I

write as a Christian I do so well aware of all that
we owe to other great religions. The best of the
Jewish tradition tells us that not even all the
weapons in the world can bring us real security:

> *A King is not saved by his army*
> *nor a warrior preserved by his strength.*
> *A vain hope for safety is the war horse;*
> *despite its power it cannot save.*

> (Psalm 33)

The Muslim faith has its Ahmadiyya movement,
which 'enjoins on every Muslim to sacrifice his
all for the protection of the weak and oppressed,
whether Muslims or not'. Hindus and Buddhists
have their own traditions of peace and non-viol-
ence. Small groups like the Baha'is have wit-
nessed to a universalist vision with consistent
courage. As we move into the twenty-first century
real believers (not quite the same thing as 'the
religious') have above all this to offer – a conviction that the world is not ours to exploit.

In the last century a tourist from America paid
a visit to a renowned Polish Rabbi named Hofetz
Chaim. He was astonished to see that the Rabbi's
home was only a simple room filled with books,
plus a table and a bench.

'Rabbi,' asked the tourist, 'where is your furni-
ture?'

'Where is yours?' replied Hofetz Chaim.

'Mine?' asked the puzzled American. 'But I'm
only passing through.'

'So am I,' said the Rabbi.

If the religions of the world could unite in reminding us that we are 'only passing through', our attitudes to many things would change radically. We live in one world, we are the trustees of what we have, and we share one humanity.

Chapter 5
Global Threats

Not long ago I accompanied an old lady to Heathrow Airport. She was on her way to settle with her daughter in Melbourne, Australia. She caught her flight at mid-morning on a Monday. On the Tuesday evening I phoned her and she was already there, unpacking and enjoying the sunshine. Ten thousand miles in twenty-four hours. It reminded me of the book I had recently read about the opening of the penal colonies in Australia in the eighteenth century and the journey the ships and prisoners had to make. The same trip to Australia then took over six months. It would be at least a year before any message got back to report safe arrival.

That we live in one small world is getting more and more obvious. What is also obvious is that the threats to the world which we now face have to have a global answer. Numerous official reports have appeared in the last ten years with the word 'common' in their titles. In 1982 the Swedish Prime Minister Olof Palme produced one on defence and the arms race called *Common Security*. In 1987 the United Nations World Commission on Environment and Development produced a report called *Our Common Future*. Common opportunities, common threats, and therefore common responses are becoming obvious.

But too many people go on thinking about the world as if we the British (or we the Russians, the Americans or anyone else) can go on planning for our lives as if what happens in our patch is all that matters. If the water tank at the top of a block of flats bursts, all the flats are threatened. If the children in one family gets measles, then all those who go to the same school will probably come out in spots as well. As I have suggested, we must have a revolution in our thinking. It's time we took our common existence seriously.

The German philosopher Schopenhauer once said, 'There are three stages in the revelation of any truth. In the first it is ridiculed, in the second it is resisted, in the third it is considered self-evident.' Ideas about global responsibility used to be thought middle-class and rather eccentric. Now they are on the edge of becoming self-evident.

Everyone knows about Aids. In this country very few people so far have known someone who has died from it. But it's well on its way to becoming a world threat which has no respect for national boundaries. By the year 2000 6 million people may have Aids, while 15 to 20 million adults and 10 million children may be infected with the human immunodeficiency virus (HIV), according to the World Health Organization. It will orphan some 10 million children in the 1990s said the UN Secretary General in his Aids Day 1990 message. Aids will be 'one of the main causes of death of US women of childbearing age in 1991', said a report in the *Washington Post*.

Aids is only one global health threat. The greatest global health threat currently lies in the militarization of our world. I've got a nice little postcard on my desk. It shows a drawing of a dinosaur – small eyes, large feet, enormous body. The text underneath says, 'Too few brains, too much armour, now extinct.' The dinosaur may be us unless we change our ideas about security. Not only does the militarization of the world cost nearly a thousand billion dollars a year, but it makes the world an increasingly insecure place in which to live. It is as if we all inhabited different rooms of the same house and imagined that the best way to be safe was to fill 'our' room with as much gunpowder as possible. The Brundtland Report clearly connected militarism and environmental dangers. Chapter eleven said: 'Among the dangers facing the environment the possibility of nuclear war or military conflict of a lesser scale involving weapons of mass destruction is undoubtedly the greatest.'

It has yet to dawn on most of us that we have reached a point in human history when wars do not have winners – only losers. It used to be believed that 'keeping the peace' meant having more ability to destroy one's neighbour than he had to destroy oneself. 'If you want peace, prepare for war,' the Romans used to say – deterrence, in short. In a famous speech in 1979 Lord Louis Mountbatten called that idea 'absolute nuclear nonsense'. The truth is that if we want peace we have to prepare for peace. This is, of course, something which we understand very well indeed within the local community. If someone on your street bangs into your car or swears at your children or plays very loud music it it *not* normal to start threatening him or her with a shotgun. If you did, it would be you who would end up in court.

New thinking is on the way, but unfortunately militaristic old thinking has a lot of influential lobbies behind it – scientists whose research jobs depend on military spending, trade unionists who are employed by defence contractors, and the defence industry itself, which is very profitable. Also, those in government know very well that presenting people with an outside threat requiring a military response very effectively unites them and silences voices of opposition. Field Marshal Hermann Goering, one of Hitler's most senior associates, is reported to have said just this at Nuremberg:

> Why, of course the people don't want war. It is the leaders who determine the policy and it is always a simple matter to drag the people along, whether it is a democracy or a Fascist dictatorship or a parliament or a communist dictatorship. All you have to do is to tell them that they are being attacked and denounce the pacifists for lack of patriotism and exposing the country to danger. It works the same in any country.

The list of global, 'common' problems is as long as you like to make it. One was dramatically underlined in 1986 when the nuclear reactor at Chernobyl burnt out and radioactive clouds wandered around Europe, dropping their deadly loads. A study carried out by the United States Department of Energy indicated that radiation from the accident could contribute to as many as 39,000 cancer deaths, most of them outside the Soviet Union.

Every schoolchild now knows about CFC gases and the ozone layer, the destruction of the rain forests, carbon dioxide and the 'greenhouse effect'. One does not have to be a research scientist to know that the world population curve is rising dramatically upwards and will reach the level of 10 billion by the middle of the next century – that's a long way from the figure of

1½ billion with which we started this one. At the same time we have treated agricultural land as if it belonged to this generation only. World fertilizer consumption has gone up from about 14 million tons in 1950 to 140 million tons today. But it is not only the land which we exploit and pollute. Nuclear waste has been dumped on the sea beds and leaks from sunken submarines. Greedy eyes are already being cast on the virgin areas of Antarctica.

So far I have not mentioned the most pressing 'common' problem of them all – and that is poverty. The UN Development Programme Report for 1990 says:

> there are still a billion people in absolute poverty; nearly 900 million adults unable to read or write; 1.75 billion without safe drinking water; around 100 million completely homeless; some 800 million who go hungry every day; 150 million children under five (one in three) who are malnourished; 14 million children who die each year before their fifth birthday.

This is the central problem. Perhaps its root cause is selfishness; and perhaps the same is true of all the other problems. It gets worse. We have an entirely unjust world economic order which makes the poor poorer with greater and greater debt burdens, while the wealthy of the developed countries (not their poor, who also exist in their millions) enjoy affluent lifestyles.

The solution to this problem has to be one which involves a new understanding of our obligations in justice. Call it a global-family justice. Economic systems which exploit the many for the benefit of the few are morally wrong, and no amount of tinkering with such systems will make them right. We need a new ethic: that of the world community. The prophet Isaiah said it all long ago to the pious of his day:

> *Is not the fast that pleases me –*
> *It is the Lord Yahweh who speaks –*
> *to break unjust fetters*
> *and undo the thongs of the yoke,*
> *to let the oppressed go free,*
> *to share your bread with the hungry*
> *and shelter the homeless poor?*

If we do not start to live together and share what we have, then there will surely be an explosion of social unrest. Archbishop Helder Camara once said that when he gave food to the poor he was called a Christian, but when he told the poor why they had no food he was called a communist. As the next century draws closer, we need more people of the Helder Camara variety to jab our consciences here in the comfortable West.

Chapter 6
Flocks of Sheep

A boy was killed not long ago at a school of which I am a Governor. There had been a fight, and this turned into a feud which resulted in the boy's death. Another boy was carrying a knife and in the heat of the moment he used it.

People seemed to be surprised at the level of violence in our society today. I'm not. In view of the fact that the media present violence as acceptable entertainment and as a legitimate means of solving problems, it is amazing that there isn't more of it. The *Star* in February 1986 surveyed TV programmes up to 9.00 p.m. on all channels each evening for a week. It was assumed that children would be doing homework or on their way to bed after that time. Some hope! In the one week of TV there were 131 killings, 22 non-fatal shootings, 21 assaults, 10 bombings and 13 riots. No one child would have seen all of this violence but each one would have got a good dose.

My point? If we are going to try to change ideas, then we have to look at the role the media play informing present ones. I've had a long ten years as General Secretary and Chairperson of CND in which to examine the media and I've learnt some hard lessons. I'm not thinking just of the values which the media presents – power, success, glamour, wealth and violence. I wonder sometimes if the media reflect the values of society or does society reflect the values of the media?

I am deeply concerned about the way in which the media, under positive political direction, can form minds on key issues – the issues which face us as we try to build a twenty-first-century world. It was Lord Northcliffe, the great Fleet Street Baron of the 1930s, who said, 'The members of the public are like a flock of sheep; they are easily led. You only have to go on repeating a thing long enough and consistently enough and they will believe it.' That sounds fairly cynical and will offend those many journalists who try to present alternative viewpoints honestly.

Sadly, after my ten years of close association with the Campaign for Nuclear Disarmament, I have to say that in my judgement Northcliffe was more or less right. For many years the public had been fed a series of dogmatic 'defence' assumptions, on the basis of which any serious discussion was meant to start. One such assumption was that people had to be divided into 'multilateralists' or 'unilateralists'. Indeed, the latter term became effectively a catch-all dismissive label.

The notion that it was possible to be both unilateralist and multilateralist at the same time, and indeed that the labels made no sense at all unless applied to specific proposals, was never allowed to surface. The real distinction, as we now know, is between those who believe in a world free of weapons of mass destruction, in which all peoples would live interdependently, and those who believe with Mrs Thatcher that 'we' will have nuclear weapons 'for the foreseeable future'. Why those who defend our 'right' to nuclear weapons are entitled to deny such 'rights' to others is never explained.

There were, of course, a whole list of other media assumptions which it was almost impossible to deal with. One was that the Soviet Union was poised to invade and occupy Western Europe. It was assumed that the Soviets had the military and political ability to do this. One famous *Times* article was illustrated by a map in which long black arrows swept across Germany, Belgium and France. This was supposed to show how Soviet tanks would reach the Channel ports. No one can fail to know now that the national differences which existed amongst Warsaw Pact countries would have made any such operations extremely unlikely, to say the least.

Nevertheless, for forty years the image of the all-powerfully malign and expansionist Soviet Union was used in the West to justify military expenditure. Only now, when the Cold War is over, comes the admission that the statistics on Soviet military strength were wildly exaggerated. In February 1991 the USA acknowledged privately that it had hugely overestimated Soviet forces. 'The margin of error was around 30,000 tanks, guns and armoured personnel carriers.' Estimates of Soviet chemical weapon stocks have dropped from 300,000 tons to 50,000 tons without a sign of embarrassment.

We must remember that even in a democracy like ours, far more open to alternative opinions than many other regimes, public opinion is a marketable commodity. Manufacturers know this perfectly well; otherwise they would not spend thousands of pounds on ten-second TV advertisements for their products. In his book, *The Power Elite* C. Wright Mills points out that

> Alongside or just below the elite there is the propagandist, the public relations man, who would control the very formation of public opinion in order to be able to include it as one more pacified item in the calculation of effective power, increased prestige, more secure wealth.

Usually the manipulation of ideas is a clever behind-the-scenes operation. Only recently, thanks to Professor Wittner of Albany University, New York, have we learnt how Prime Minister Harold MacMillan secretly mobilized some of the Bishops of the Church of England and the BBC against the influence of CND in the sixties.

Occasionally the manipulation is so blatant that it is counter-productive. An example of this is the persistent allegation which used to be made that CND was receiving millions of roubles from the USSR. It became a bad joke. Another example is the article by a Yossef Bodansky which was published in the respected magazine, *Janes' Defence Weekly* in January 1986. It made the most preposterous claims about the women who were then camped at the Greenham Common cruise missile base. Those women were already no strangers to media manipulation. Bodansky claimed, 'The Soviet Union has maintained a secret detachment of female Spetsnaz special forces in the area . . . since the deployment of . . . cruise missiles there in December 1983.' The thought of these agents sitting over campfires in the mud and trying to pass themselves off as British peaceniks simply made me laugh.

This amazing story, unsupported by a shred of evidence, went the rounds of all the serious papers as well as the tabloids. ITN even managed to produce a mock-up of a Spetsnaz training camp somewhere in the Soviet Union, which was shown on the evening news. Then the story, too ridiculous even for the Hawks to believe, just vanished. No one apologized, the episode was over, Bodansky could not be found. Clearly one of the image manipulators had just gone too far. They are much more dangerous when they don't.

Does all this have relevance to our thinking about the oncoming century? I believe it has a great deal of relevance. The Sacred Cows of militarism, nationalism and economic power are going to have to be moved from their Sacred stalls if there is to be a new world order. A whole range of people are going to find that the power they have wielded and the privileges they have enjoyed are threatened as we move to a new interdependent world in which there is enough for everyone's need but not enough for everyone's greed. Those who propose a radical departure from the traditional ways of distributing power and wealth are never going to be popular with those who live privileged lives because of the way society is organized. So if you decide to start on the road of radical change do not expect that life will be easy. It will be made quite difficult. In some countries it could mean imprisonment and persecution. In Britain your name might well go on a blacklist – after that you may find it very difficult to get a job. But whatever the difficulties, you are guaranteed an interesting and useful life.

Chapter 7
International Structures

Whatever one's views about the Gulf War and its aftermath, one thing is perfectly clear. The United Nations is now on everyone's lips. The organization which was ignored for far too long has suddenly come right into the centre spotlight of the world stage. Those governments which fought Iraq – principally the American and British ones – did so on the grounds that this action was endorsed by Security Council resolutions. People, such as myself, who were against the war also claimed the authority of the United Nations, through its Charter.

The Charter has become a key text. The odd thing is that so few people have ever seen it. Few of those have ever studied it. The powerful nations have at different times both used and ignored the UN so as to protect their own interests. In 1986 the UN called for an International Year of Peace, but in Britain that call fell on entirely deaf ears. The Government of the day did exactly nothing by way of response. I cannot say that over the years non-governmental organizations have been much more interested in UN activity. Some have seen the UN as a self-protecting body of supposedly independent states which, despite the Universal Declaration of Human Rights of 1948, can still do what they like within their own borders. That, after all, is what the Charter said in Article 2.7:

> Nothing contained in the present Charter shall authorize the United Nations to intervene in matters which are essentially within the domestic jurisdiction of any state . . .

So terrorism or civil war has continued in Northern Ireland in its most recent phase for over twenty years, and still the international community can have no official voice in the solution of the problem.

Others have suspected the UN of being no more than a Cold War battlefield. There is actually much truth in the accusation, although Mikhail Gorbachev has greatly changed that perception, not least in a remarkable speech to the UN in 1988.

Whatever the previous doubts, we do now have a remarkable moment of opportunity. Whatever the weaknesses of the UN – and they are many – its very existence is a fragile miracle. It is not the only international structure. All kinds of different organizations, from churches to trade unions, form their own networks which interlock people and bypass national structures. The European Community is now more than an economic institution and the all-Europe 'Helsinki Process' is beginning to have a life of its own. The suggestion that the dictator of Iraq should be tried as a war criminal implies a recognition that we need an international legal structure which can deal with individual delinquents. Perhaps there should be a world criminal court? The United Nations is still, however, our principle international body, and if we are not to return to chaos, we have to make it work.

The chief problem is simply ignorance. During a speech at a fringe meeting at the Labour Party Conference in Blackpool in 1990, I happened to hold up a small, blue eighty-seven-page booklet – it was a copy of the United Nations Charter. A television producer came to me afterwards with his camera crew and asked with respect, 'Is that the Charter of the United Nations?' I said it was. With an air of amazement he asked me if I would hold it up and be photographed with it. I had the feeling that he thought I had produced something as rare as the Dead Sea Scrolls. In a sense I had. Since then, time after time in schools and colleges I have been impressed by the fact that the UN Charter is unknown country to all sorts of educated people. This is an extraordinary situation. Education at its best must be about learning to live together. But too little is actually known about the organization which was created for that purpose in 1945 and which had its first General Assembly meeting in our own London Methodist Central Hall in Westminster in 1946.

Even today the preamble to the Charter is inspiring reading:

> We the peoples ... determined to save succeeding generations from the scourge of war ... to reaffirm faith in fundamental rights ... to promote social progress and better standards of life in larger freedom ... have resolved to combine our efforts to accomplish these aims.

The United Nations did not have the major weaknesses of its predecessor, the League of Nations. All the great powers became members (although, because of American pressure, communist China was excluded until 1971). Further, under Chapter VII of the Charter the UN was actually given military teeth. In theory it was not only the world's peace keeper, but it could also be the world's first peace enforcer. However, the Military Staff Committee called for by Article 47 has never had a real existence, and the Cold War made genuine Security Council agreement on such matters impossible.

The why's and wherefores of the United Nations remain mysteries to the vast majority of the public. They don't know what the Security

Council can do, they don't know what the powers of the General Assembly are, and they don't know what the authority of the International Court of Justice is, even if they know that there is such a court. They don't know who appoints the Secretary General and they haven't the slightest idea how much the whole operation costs. Most, I suspect, think it is extremely expensive. But in fact Britain's annual contribution to the United Nations would not buy half a dozen Tornado aircraft. By comparison with the one trillion (a thousand billion) dollars the world manages to spent on war every year, the one billion dollars of the General Budget of the UN (one thousandth of the amount spent on war) seems a very poor joke.

If ignorance about the UN's main structures is considerable, ignorance about its specialized agencies and other organs is even worse. Yet without the work which they do the world would be a very much unhappier place. The World Health Organization, the Food and Agriculture Organization, the United Nations Environmental Programme and so many others including the unassuming Universal Postal Union and the World Meteorological Organization are all weaving the threads which help to interconnect us on this planet.

It is high time that we started to take the UN seriously. In September 1990 Eduard Shevardnadze, then Soviet Foreign Minister, said about the United Nations, 'Wiping off grime left by the Cold War, we see a work of collective wisdom – a centre for harmonizing the activities of nations.' If we are going to make the peoples of the world concerned about the effective working of the United Nations, they must be both informed and involved. UN Information Offices around the world work with ludicrously small budgets. Excellent printed material like the UN World Disarmament Campaign Wall Chart on the costs of the arms race is available not in tens of thousands of copies but only in tens and twenties. If we are serious about the UN we will be pushing our governments to take it seriously in financial terms. Its education programmes should be given a high priority. If there is to be a National Core Curriculum in schools in the UK, then the Charter and world-wide work of the UN has to figure prominently in it.

There are other practical reforms which ought to be made. At the moment this country is represented at the United Nations by a civil servant who is directly accountable only to the government which appoints him (so far no her!). If we want democratic involvement, this has to change. If Northern Ireland's ministers are answerable in Parliament to questions from all parties, then we also have a right to be represented on a regular basis at the United Nations by a Minister of the Crown. If what goes on in the UN is important, then the public and not just Parliament must know about it. We can afford to spend millions on programmes of health education, for instance, and even on the privatization of gas and electricity. We are not too poor to be able to afford programmes designed to inform the public about the work which is going on at the United Nations.

People need not only to be informed but also to be involved. In that 1988 address Mikhail Gorbachev said, 'The idea of convening on a regular basis, under the auspices of the United Nations, an assembly of public organizations deserves attention.' Why should there be such an assembly? Ideally this second chamber would be formed on a democratic basis, at least in the long term. At the moment genuine democracies are in a minority. However in the European Parliament we already experience a democratic system which produces a regional forum. There would be a long way to go before a UN second chamber could be elected in this way. Nevertheless at the moment many 'public organizations' as Gorbachev has called them – including medical associations, trade unions and youth groups – have a popular base and do not represent particular states. The United Nations already has an organized system of Non-Governmental Organizations, and their role would be increased if some of them sat in a second chamber with the right to initiate proposals and to comment on resolutions under discussion.

Of course, there would be problems. Reforms

like the ones we have mentioned would be ridiculed initially. That would be no surprise. George Bernard Shaw once said, 'Some men see things as they are and ask "Why?" I dream things that never were and ask "Why not?" ' The UN needs a few more people who are willing to face future opportunities and ask, 'Why not?' It is important that they should. It is my own conviction, not shared by all UN supporters, that 1990 and 1991 have seen the remaining superpower hijack the United Nations, forcing it to agree to an unnecessary war. The image of the UN will have been damaged for many. The humiliation of its Secretary General has been plain to see. Education about the UN and the reform of its structures are now more necessary than ever as the next century looms on the horizon. The UN's fiftieth birthday in 1995 might be a target date for completed reformation.

Chapter 8
Suggestions for Action

A nineteenth-century author once said, 'Words that do not lead to action had better be suppressed.' It doesn't much matter who put those words into circulation. The idea is an old and sensible one.

I have not written this short book in order to entertain you but rather in order to share with you my conviction that we humans are not doomed simply to watch history unfold but to do something about the direction it takes. Sometimes people look down their noses when they hear the word 'activist', as if to be an activist was rather unseemly. I believe it to be essential. We had better start to be active if we are to avoid some of the global perils which we now face.

The difficulty in thinking about our entry into the twenty-first century is that the problems are too great. If I were suggesting a campaign to get local street cleaning improved or a day nursery established, then those would be manageable challenges. But moving from a divided world, based on out-of-date ideas about national sovereignty, to a world in which global citizenship is the framework into which other loyalties have to fit, seems overwhelmingly difficult.

Difficult it is, of course, but there is no reason why the change cannot be handled if there is sufficient collective courage and determination. Human beings have adapted to other great changes. It wasn't easy to get people to accept that the earth actually goes round the sun and not vice versa. It wasn't easy to bring the slave trade to an end, to get votes for women, or to create public health and education services. That we are economically interdependent is quite a new idea, and so too is the view that development aid is a matter of justice, not charity; but people are beginning to accept both concepts. It is certainly quite revolutionary that there should be a European Court of Human Rights to which aggrieved citizens can take their governments, but it exists. Point one is therefore not to let the size of the task discourage you.

Point two is to realize that you are not going to have to do the job on your own. Your part, like anyone else's, will be quite small. The change in ideas, as great as any Copernican sun-and-earth revolution, is going to be the result of a collective effort which is already well under way. The Charter of the United Nations, though largely still unknown, is already over forty years old. Its vision has inspired the lives of countless people unknown to us.

Point three is to remember that change does not happen in an even-measured way so that progress can be noted and self-confidence assured. Social change is rather more like a bon-fire. Nothing seems to happen for a long time except signs of smouldering. Then suddenly flames leap up and for a while the fire races. Then it goes back to smouldering before starting up again later on. We must pace ourselves. The frenetic doomsday activist rushing from meeting to meeting, more committed apparently than anyone else, may be a caricature, but he or she does exist. Such people burn out their activity rather rapidly. When it comes to social change my money is firmly on the tortoise rather than on the hare. Do what you can where you are at the speed you can manage. Have some fun at the same time *and* persevere.

Point four is not to try to do everything. Choose the issue in which you are interested and get on with that, with many a sympathetic sideways look at those working on other issues. After all, like spokes on a wheel, they all comp-lement and converge. Sometimes people tell me that I should stop working on the perils that result from the militarization of our world and rechannel my efforts, for instance, into solving population problems, since they are 'more important'. There is no point in this sort of redirection. Ninety per cent of those fellow human beings who are free from desperate poverty and have the leisure to work for social change nevertheless simply take life as it is. It is amongst the inactive majority that we should be recruiting new members, not amongst those already busy with important campaigns.

What does all this boil down to in practice? It means working to change the way in which people see our world. My generation learned history in a way that may surprise this one. At school we each had a white card and on it were printed all the names and dates of the kings and queens of England. In another column there were the dates of all the English battles. These facts we had to learn by heart, and I can still recite some of them now. What the Chinese or the Slavs or the Australian Aborigines were up to when we were engaged in the Battle of Hastings in 1066 I have not the slightest idea. What other world religions were doing while Western Christendom experienced the Reformation I never thought to enquire. How the Muslims or the Jews interpreted their history was not on our agenda. We did not have a global vision but an imperial one. It is a great joy to me to see how schools today are trying to put their teaching into a global framework of respect for the best in other faiths and other cultures.

International travel has never been easier than

it is now, but the results can be very superficial. I am not sure that it does much for one's global vision to go on a package holiday and just sit on a hot beach somewhere getting a suntan. But a visit to another country, when you have done some background reading about its history and problems, you have made some effort to be able to say in another language more than 'How much are the postcards?' and you have planned in advance some contact with local people, is valuable indeed. Travel is not, in any event, a one-way process. To Britain alone thousands of students, business people, refugees and holiday-makers come on a long- or short-term basis. How we welcome them is an indication of our international attitudes. I remember with affection and gratitude a lady in my first parish who used to hold a regular coffee evening in her flat on Wednesday evenings. To Mrs Mason I could always take any foreigner and make him or her feel at home. Those Wednesday evenings never made the headlines or got her to a Buckingham Palace Garden Party, but as I look back nearly forty years I realize that Mrs Mason was putting into action in a practical way the ideas that I am talking about now.

Coffee evenings? I can hear my radical friends snorting with indignation. 'Is this all that he is suggesting?' they ask. Of course not. But the art of being really radical is to be able to bring others along with you. One-world ideas are not only for the esoteric and politically advanced. They have got to spread amongst ordinary church congregations, trade union branches, farmers' clubs, local choirs and sports associations. When ordinary people come to believe that United Nations Day (24th October) is a more important event on our annual calendar than bank holidays or royal birthdays, then we can claim to have made some progress.

Progress, of course, has already been made. There are tens of thousands of ordinary people involved in organizations like Amnesty International, Friends of the Earth, Oxfam, Christian Aid, Greenpeace, the Red Cross and the United Nations Association. Thousands of local authorities are twinned with partnership cities and towns in other countries on a worldwide and not just a European basis. The exploitation that our present world economic system involves is starting to be understood.

One danger is that those who do not want us to move away from the nation state vision and towards the global one will try to co-opt such organizations and movements to their own ends. In their view it is fine to be fighting for human rights as long as it is other states that are being criticized; it is fine to oppose pollution as long as it is other countries' pollution; it is fine to support the United Nations as long as you don't comment critically on our level of funding or voting record; it is fine to oppose militarization in general as long as you don't criticize our military machine; it is fine to support international law in theory, as long as you don't try to make it condemn the idea of 'peace' being based on the threat of mass destruction.

In Britain over the past forty years the key symbol of nationalism has been the British nuclear Bomb. Ernest Bevin even said in 1947 that he had to have one with 'a bloody Union Jack on top of it'. It is no surprise that the forces of official hatred and contempt have been brought to bear against those of us who have opposed it. Power does not give up easily. Massive vested interests will oppose moves which will take us away from the fragmentation of our world, since this state of affairs has given them enormous power. Those who set out on the global road need not expect to have an easy ride. No matter. Ideas like the internationalist perspective have their own time. As we approach the next century the notion that we are one people and that we have to build the structures of justice and community within which we can all live is becoming more and more self-evident. Our task is to work to ensure that this view of the world becomes the obvious one.

Chapter 9
Signposts

In 1940 Vera Brittain, one of the most articulate, hardworking and determined believers in peace and world order of her generation, made a return visit to Oxford. The Second World War was in full swing, the League of Nations, upon which Vera had built her hopes, was discredited, and peace seemed a long way off. Her wartime autobiography, *England's Hour* contains these words which she wrote during that Oxford trip: 'The world of men, and especially the world of statesmen, loves the pursuit of power by the old destructive methods far too well to be readily dissuaded from it by a few idealists with disconcerting dreams of a City of God.'

The same feelings are in my heart as I write. The war to remove Iraq from Kuwait ended a few months ago. Tens of thousands of young Iraqi conscript soldiers and unknown numbers of Iraqi civilians died. The agony of the Kurds

and the Shias goes on. The Palestinians are
further from justice than they were when the war
started. Incalculable damage has been done to
the environment by the oil fires started by the
bombing and by the arson of the dictator Saddam
Hussein. Who knows how many billions of dollars the war cost both sides? We will never know
whether Saddam might have been forced by non-
violent means to give up Kuwait, because such
means were never given a chance to work.

With Vera Brittain I have seen the pursuit of
power, no doubt in a just cause, 'by the old
destructive methods'. It is a time for realism.
Those who dream dreams about the future have
much to do to turn those dreams into reality.
Those who put their faith in the United Nations,
as Vera put hers in the League of Nations, have
to acknowledge how easily such international
bodies can be co-opted by major military powers.

But if in one way I am depressed, in another
I am profoundly encouraged. Vera Brittain never
gave up. Throughout the Second World War she
wrote a monthly newsletter to encourage and
support all her scattered 'peace' friends. She
opposed both plaster-bombing and the call for
unconditional surrender, and her unpopularity
soared in official circles. After the war she was
amongst the first to organize relief for the starv-
ing Germans. She did not give up.

It is because of the hundreds of much less
well-known people whom I have met – people

with the same vision and the same determination as Vera had – that I believe we can move in to the twenty-first century in hope.

A couple of years ago I helped to pay for a headstone for an unmarked grave in a South London cemetery. It was the grave of Charles Cobb, a Christian tea merchant's clerk who had refused military service in World War One. He was sent to Dartmoor prison, where he was cruelly treated. He was released after the war was over, broken in health but not in spirit. A few weeks later, in early 1919, he died because of the treatment he had been given, buried unknown, in a pauper's grave. It took over sixty years for local peace people to find out about him and to spread his story. They set up a head-stone at his grave, and the local press reported it. His courage has had a powerful message long after he was supposed to be forgotten.

We have got to value and learn from those who have managed to say 'No' – sometimes at great personal cost – to the evils of their gener-ations. We must resist the wrongs of today if we are to move on to tomorrow. That is exactly what the women of Greenham Common did, and they did it effectively. Hated by the respectable estab-lishment, they paid a hard price in abuse, misrep-resentation and physical violence. One day their year-after-year witness in the mud and the cold against nuclear-weapon barbarity will get the credit it deserves. Theirs was a very powerful 'No.'

Then, across the Atlantic, there is the case of Bob Aldridge, a prosperous, successful Lockheed engineer who was working on missile guidance systems. He came to realize that the pin-point accuracy of those systems could only have one purpose: to enable the missiles to deliver a warhead which could destroy opposing missiles before they were fired. In other words he was creating a war-fighting first-strike capability; the weapons were designed not for defence but for attack. Even though he had a large family to support, he resigned. His career in the weapons industry was finished. He set off to follow his conscience and in doing so inspired thousands.

I sometimes wonder if it was Aldridge's example which provoked Pope John Paul II to make the issue of scientific refusal central to his message to the Pontifical Academy of Sciences in November 1983. In that message he said:

When, in a particular historical situation, it is all but inevitable that a certain form of scientific research will be used for purposes of aggression, the scientist must make a choice that will enable him to work for the good of the people, for the building up of peace. By refusing certain fields of research, inevitably destined, in the concrete historical circumstances, for deadly purposes, the scientists of the whole world ought to be united in a common readiness to disarm science and to form a providential force for peace.

I have in the past ten years with CND been in a very privileged position. At close quarters I have seen the devotion and perseverance of so many people who never hit the headlines – those who have campaigned against nuclear weapons, against the arms trade, for the legal right to redirect to humanitarian purposes the proportion of their taxes now earmarked for military defence (the so-called 'Peace Tax'), for an effective United Nations and for a world in which we will turn swords into ploughshares. Pensioners, children, ex-service men and women . . . people beyond number. I have hundreds of photographs of ordinary, caring people, many of whom, in their friendships and career prospects, have suffered a great deal for their convictions. Some have see the inside of prison. This is what gives me the greatest hope. The old structures still remain, but there is a new people on the way.

My personal hero is an Austrian farmer who was unknown in his lifetime, but who is now recognized as a man of integrity and courage. One day the Catholic Church may even call him a saint. Franz Jägerstätter, a married man with three small children, was called up to join Hitler's army in 1943. Despite the advice of his parish priest and his bishop, uneducated Franz just went on saying that Hitler's wars were unjust and that he would take no part in them. Though told by many that what he was doing would make no difference, he stood by his principles. He persisted in saying that there were some things the State could not make him do. The Nazi regime had no room for conscientious objectors. The legal process did not take too long. Finally, alone and isolated, Franz was beheaded in a Berlin prison on 9th August 1943. That should have been the end of an insignificant person like Franz.

But the story of his 'No' has spread. Kurt Waldheim, Austrian President and former United Nations Secretary General, is now in disgrace for his willingness to participate in Hitler's wars. Jägerstätter is now honoured, and not only in Austria. To the War Memorial in the little Austrian village of St Radegund his name also has been added. From all over the world people now come to pay their respects in the churchyard where his ashes are buried.

We can all find our different sources of inspiration, and we will need them. A new world order is not going to come prepacked off the shelf. We will have to work and suffer for it. Rose Macaulay, a contemporary of Vera Brittain, once wrote a lovely fantasy called *The Towers of Trebizond*. At one point the central character runs up against a very nationalistic Turkish girl who is passionately devoted to her country. Then the heroine reflects, 'I went on musing about why it was thought better and higher to love one's country than one's county, or town or village or house. Perhaps because it was larger. But then it would be still better to love one's continent, and best of all to love one's planet.' We are going to have to do much more about loving the planet than we have done so far if we are to make sense of the twenty-first century.